READING GUIDES **LYCÉE**

CAHIER D'ACCOMPAGNEMENT
à la lecture de l'œuvre intégrale

The Curious Incident of the Dog in the Night-Time

Mark Haddon

Corinne Escales
IA-IPR, Académie de Versailles

Nathan

Où trouver Les ressources de mon manuel ?

Toutes les ressources élèves (audios, vidéos, activités interactives) sont accessibles via Nathan live ou sur le site compagnon :

Nathan live ! NOUVEAU !

Flashez les pages directement avec Nathan Live pour accéder aux ressources gratuitement !

Nathan live!

1. Téléchargez **l'application gratuite Nathan live** disponible sur votre smartphone ou votre tablette (Appstore, GooglePlay)
2. Ouvrez l'application. Flashez les pages de l'ouvrage où apparaît un picto en plaçant votre appareil au-dessus de la page. Vous accédez directement à la ressource !

(!) L'application nécessite une connexion Internet

Site compagnon → **lyceen.nathan.fr/reading-guides**

Direction éditoriale : Marie Lucas
Édition : Seonaid Cruickshank, Cyrielle Massieux
Conception de la couverture : Julie Lannes
Conception de la maquette : Julie Lannes, Clémentine Largant
Illustrations : Philippe Gady
Mise en pages : Patrick Droit

ISBN : 978-2-09-178110-5

TABLE OF CONTENTS

DISCOVERING

BUILD YOUR PORTFOLIO BAC

Nathan Live

Listen to extracts, watch videos, visit websites with Nathan Live.

MARK HADDON

Mark Haddon was born in Northampton, England, in 1963. He is a novelist and illustrator. His first published books were for children. *The Curious Incident of the Dog in the Night-Time* is his most famous novel. It was published in 2003 as both a children's edition and an adult edition.

Complete the information about Mark Haddon using these links.

Site A short biography on the British Council site.

Site Find information about his work on his site.

Site An article about prizes won by the book on the *Guardian* site.

MARK HADDON

Children's/Young adult fiction

....

....

....

....

Adult fiction

....

....

....

....

Poetry

....

....

Screenplays

....

....

....

Prizes

....

....

....

....

....

Main topics

....

....

....

....

....

Information about his life

....

....

....

....

MARK HADDON ON *THE CURIOUS INCIDENT*

I've always regretted that the phrase "Asperger Syndrome" appeared on the cover of *Curious Incident* when it was first published. Mostly because the central conceit was that Christopher himself had written the book (for a long time it had the dull but accurate working title, Christopher's Book) and "Asperger Syndrome" is not a phrase he uses. In the book he refers to himself only as "someone who has Behavioural Problems".

I prefer the wry humour in these words. I like the way it gently mocks the diagnostic medical language. I like the way it includes all of us (who doesn't have behavioural problems?). But I like it most of all because it is Christopher's own phrase. Labels tell us very little about the person who has been labelled and a lot about the people doing the labelling. If you want to find out who someone is, just ask them. [...]

I'm in favour of anything that introduces a little more empathy into the world, but I'd like to fight the corner for *Curious* simply as a novel. Of course, it's about disability and our attitudes towards it, but it's about many other things as well: mathematics, families, Sherlock Holmes, truth, bravery, Swindon, railways...

It's also a novel about the act of reading. It contains huge gaps that readers fill without noticing. Christopher, for example, never says what he looks like, the clothes he wears, the way his hair is cut, whether he is skinny or fat, tall or short. In spite of this most readers have a vivid image of him. And this, I suspect, is one of the many reasons why so many of them feel a peculiar sense of ownership about the book, for when they close the final page they have had an experience which is, to a large extent, of their own making.

If I was being contentious I might say that *Curious* is not really about Christopher at all. Christopher is an outsider, and novelists are drawn to outsiders of all kinds – Robinson Crusoe, Raskolnikov, Holden Caulfield, Jane Eyre, Benjy Compson... - because they grant us a privileged position from which we are able to look back at ourselves.

If I was being particularly contentious I might say that *Curious* is not really about Christopher at all. It's about us.

penguin.co.uk, 2015

1 **Read the article and explain what Mark Haddon has always regretted.**

2 **Sum up what the *The Curious Incident of the Dog in the Night-Time* is about.**

1 **Look at the book cover and react. Make hypotheses about the story.**

....

....

....

....

....

....

....

....

....

TOOLBOX
- garden fork
- impale = pierce with a sharp instrument

2 **curious:** ***1.*** interested in learning about people or things around you. ***2.*** strange and unusual.
After you read the novel, comment on why the word "curious" is well-chosen to speak about it.

....

....

....

....

....

....

....

....

....

3 **"The curious incident of the dog in the night-time" is a quote from the Sherlock Holmes story "Silver Blaze". What other clues does the title give about the genre of the novel?**

....

....

....

....

....

....

....

....

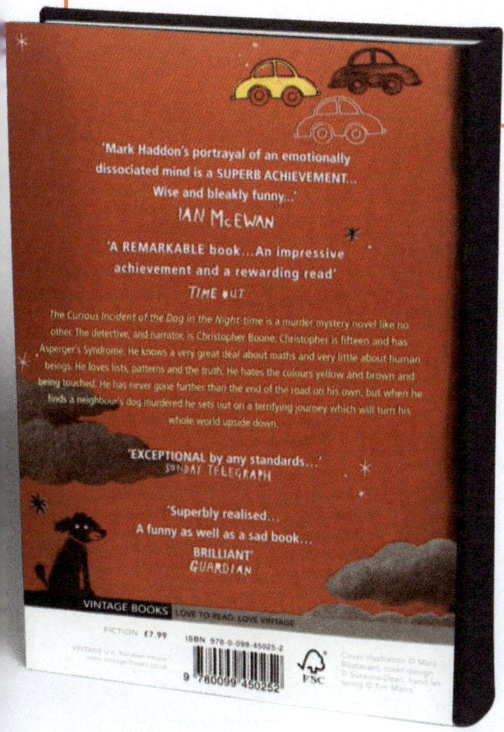

FOCUS ON...

"Silver Blaze" (1892)
by Sir Conan Doyle
is one of the most popular Sherlock Holmes short stories. It contains the title of the book:

[...] ***Gregory (Scotland Yard detective):*** *Is there any other point to which you would wish to draw my attention?*

Holmes: *To the curious incident of the dog in the night-time.*

Gregory: *The dog did nothing in the night-time.*

Holmes: *That was the curious incident.* [...]

4 **Read the back cover blurb. Highlight information about the genre (in red), the main character (in blue), what happened (in green) and what he is going to do (in yellow).**

The Curious Incident of the Dog in the Night-Time is a murder mystery novel like no other. The detective, and narrator, is Christopher Boone. Christopher is fifteen and has Asperger's Syndrome. He knows a very great deal about maths and very little about human beings. He loves lists, patterns and the truth. He hates the colours yellow and brown and being touched. He has never gone further than the end of the road on his own, but when he finds a neighbour's dog murdered he sets out on a terrifying journey which will turn his world upside down.

Discovering the characters

▶ **As you read along, complete the information about the main characters and add the links between them.**

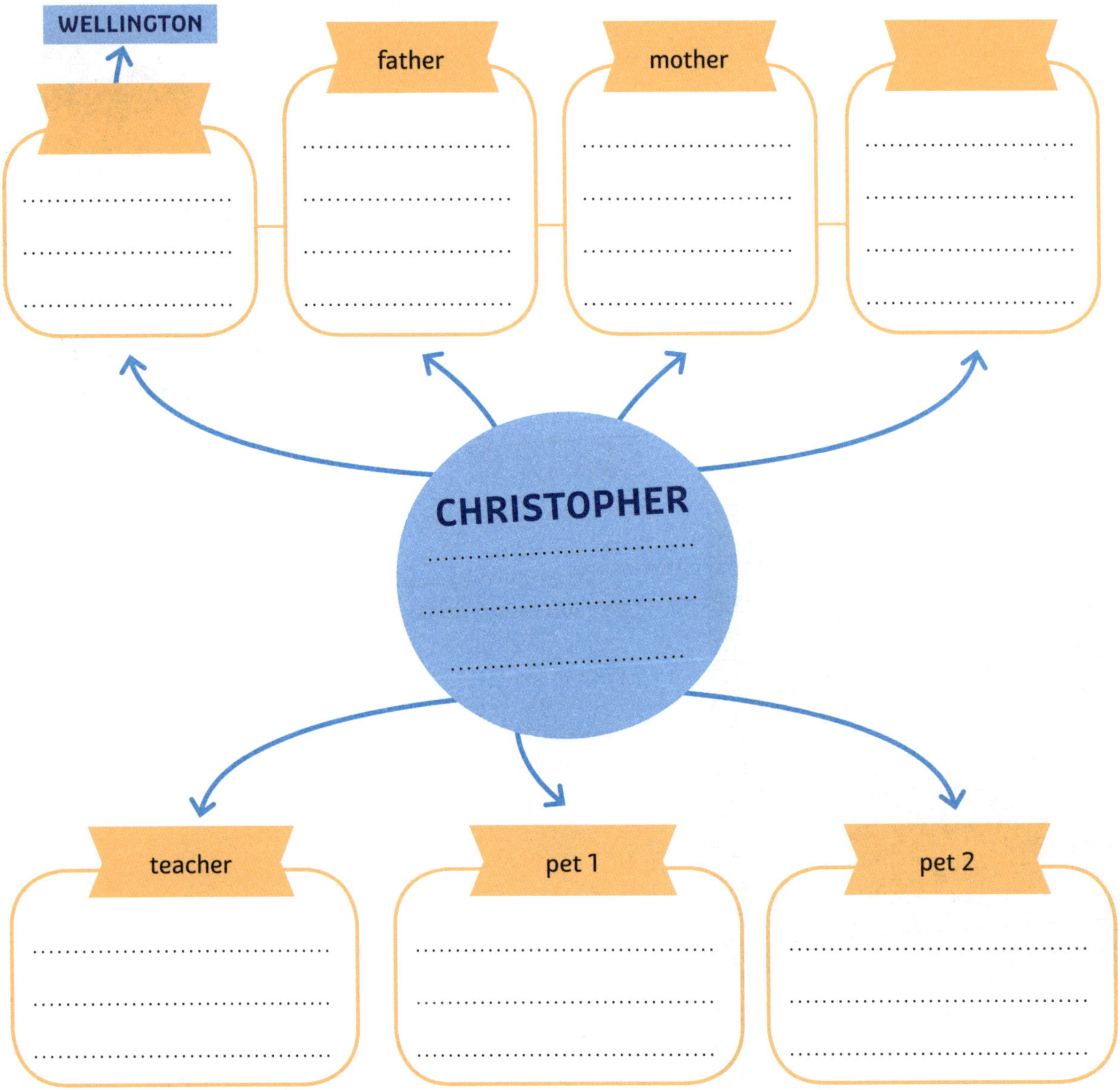

Your task

You are a young journalist for *Science Focus* in charge of writing an article on Christopher Boone, 35 years-old, who is a brilliant mathematician who has won the Fields Medal. As you contacted him to know more about his life and family, he gave you a book entitled *The Curious Incident of the Dog in the Night-Time*. You decide to open it to know more about him.

First, you read through the chapters and you are struck by chapter numbering: 2, 3, 5, 7, 11, etc. What logic is used?

Piqued by curiosity, you start reading...

PART 1

Christopher

Read the beginning of the novel (Chapter 2) and note down the information about the characters.

Extract 1

It was 7 minutes after midnight. The dog was lying on the grass in the middle of the lawn in front of Mrs Shears' house. Its eyes were closed. It looked as if it was running on its side, the way dogs run when they think they are chasing a cat in a dream. But the dog was not running or asleep. The dog was dead. There was a garden fork sticking out of the dog. The points of the fork must have gone all the way through the dog and into the ground because the fork had not fallen over. I decided that the dog was probably killed with the fork because I could not see any other wounds[1] in the dog and I do not think you would stick a garden fork into a dog after it had died for some reason, like cancer for example, or a road accident. But I could not be certain about this.

I went through Mrs Shears' gate, closing it behind me. I walked onto her lawn and knelt beside the dog. I put my hand on the muzzle of the dog. It was still warm.

The dog was called Wellington. It belonged to Mrs Shears who was our friend. She lived on the opposite side of the road, two houses to the left.

Wellington was a poodle[2]. Not one of the small poodles that have hairstyles, but a big poodle. It had curly black fur, but when you got close you could see that the skin underneath the fur was a very pale yellow, like chicken.

I stroked Wellington and wondered who had killed him, and why.

1. injuries 2. *caniche*

NOTE BOX

....

1 Fill in the card about the crime scene.

Place:	....
Victim (animal, breed, name):	....
Weapon:	....
Is it definitely a crime?	❐ yes ❐ no
Why?	....

2 **Draw the crime scene in the neighbourhood. Identify the houses with the names of the inhabitants.**

3 **Read the last sentence again: what do you think is going to happen in the novel?**

....

....

....

....

GRAMMAR LAB

Probability and certainty

a **Observe the two sentences below. Which one expresses probability in the past? certainty in the past? Tick the correct answer.**

1. *The points of the fork must have gone all the way through the dog and into the ground because the fork had not fallen over.* ❐ probability ❐ certainty

2. *I decided that the dog was probably killed with the fork because I could not see any other wounds in the dog.* ❐ probability ❐ certainty

b **Rephrase:**

Sentence 1 with an adverb:

....

....

Sentence 2 with a modal:

....

....

FOCUS ON... Whodunnits

A **whodunnit** is a mystery fiction that keeps the criminal's identity secret until the very end. The aim of the novel is to discover the identity of this criminal. *The Hound of the Baskervilles* by Sir Arthur Conan Doyle is a famous whodunnit.

a **Explain the word "whodunnit".**

b **Give two titles of whodunnits from English literature.**

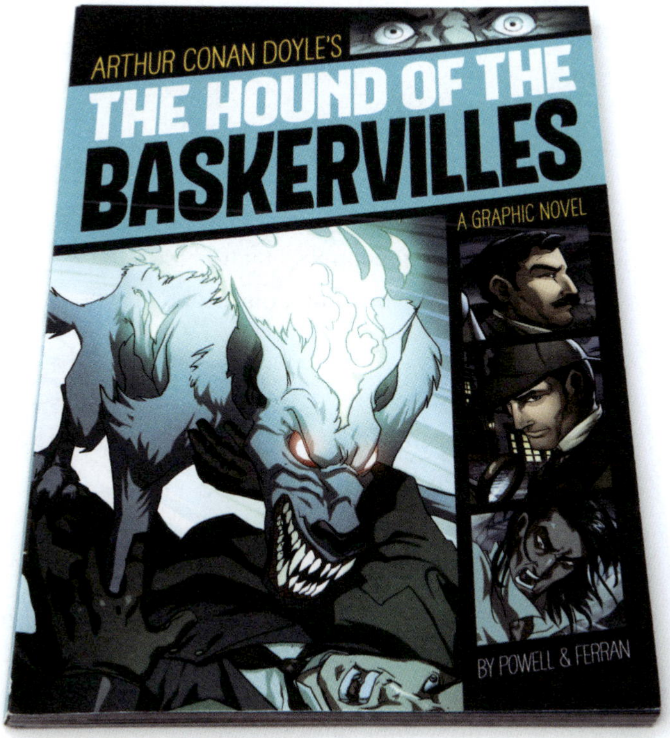

4 **Say why *The Curious Incident* starts like a whodunnit.**

WORD LAB

Crime fiction

- **Brainstorm the lexical field of whodunnits. You can continue adding words as you read the novel.**

crime • weapon • ...

5 Check your understanding

- **Tick true or false.**

	True	False
a. Wellington is Christopher's poodle.	❒	❒
b. The dog was killed at night.	❒	❒
c. Christopher is disgusted by the corpse of the dog.	❒	❒
d. Christopher wants to know who killed Wellington.	❒	❒

Read the text from Chapter 3 and take notes about Christopher.

Extract 2

My name is Christopher John Francis Boone. I know all the countries of the world and their capital cities and every prime number up to 7,507.

Eight years ago, when I first met Siobhan[1], she showed me the picture

and I knew it meant 'sad', which is what I felt when I found the dead dog.

Then she showed me this picture

and I knew it meant 'happy', like when I'm reading about the Apollo space missions, or when I am still awake at three or four in the morning and I can walk up and down the street and pretend that I am the only person in the whole world.

Then she drew some more pictures

but I was unable to say what these meant.

I got Siobhan to draw lots of these faces and then write down next to them exactly what they meant. I kept the piece of paper in my pocket and took it out when I didn't understand what someone was saying. But it was very difficult to decide which of the diagrams was most like the face they were making because people's faces move very quickly.

When I told Siobhan that I was doing this, she got out a pencil and another piece of paper and said it probably made people feel very

and then she laughed. So I tore the original piece of paper up and threw it away. And Siobhan apologised. And now if I don't know what someone is saying I ask them what they mean or I walk away.

1. Irish female name pronounced: ʃəˈvaːn

NOTE BOX

WORD LAB

Adjectives and emotions

a **Focus on the emoticons shown by Siobhan. Associate each emoticon with an adjective:**

astonished • doubtful • uncomfortable • malicious • ironic

1. .... 2. .... 3. .... 4. .... 5. ....

b **Draw emoticons corresponding to these adjectives.**

1. ashamed **2.** joyful **3.** disappointed **4.** fearful

1 **What does the scene reveal about the narrator's ability to express his feelings?**

....

....

2 **a. What is common to geography, mathematics and astronomy for the narrator?**

....

....

b. How does the narrator convey his feelings towards these three subjects throughout the novel? You can browse the novel quickly and find visual elements:

Geography: ....

....

Mathematics: ....

....

Astronomy: ....

....

3 **Guess who Siobhan may be.**

....

....

....

FOCUS ON... Asperger syndrome

Asperger syndrome (AS) is a disorder characterised by some difficulties in social interaction, restricted interests, desire for sameness, distinctive strengths such as attention to detail.

In 2013 Asperger syndrome and other previously separate types of autism folded into one umbrella diagnosis of "**autism spectrum disorder**".

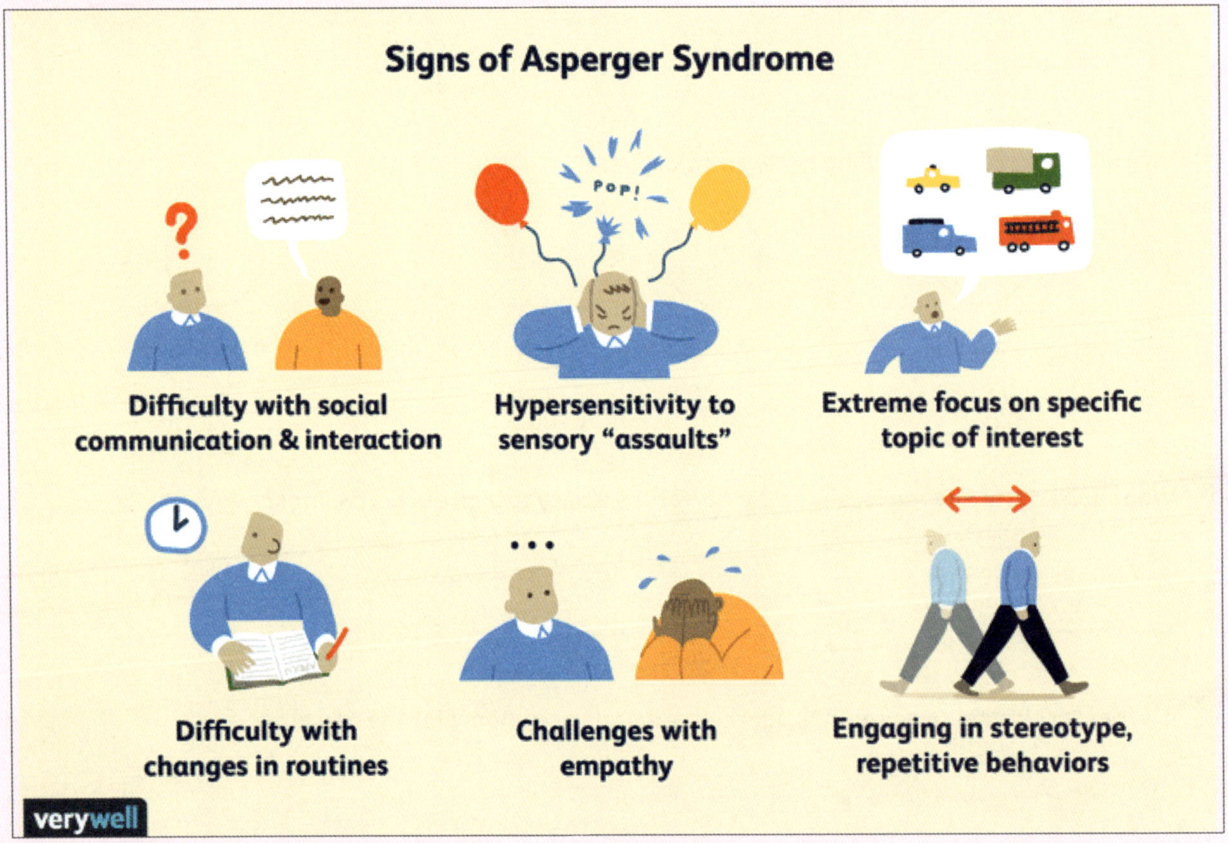

4 Check your understanding

● **Tick true or false.**

	True	False
a. *The Curious Incident* is a third-person narrative.	❒	❒
b. Christopher is able to understand all the emoticons.	❒	❒
c. Christopher does not express any emotions.	❒	❒
d. Christopher wants to understand people's emotions.	❒	❒
e. Drawing emotions helps Christopher.	❒	❒

READ ON

Now read the novel until Chapter 23. What happens to Christopher?

Read the text from Chapter 23 and learn more about Christopher.

Extract 3

When I got to the police station they made me take the laces out of my shoes and empty my pockets at the front desk in case I had anything in them that I could use to kill myself or escape or attack a policeman with.

The sergeant behind the desk had very hairy hands and he had bitten his nails so much that they had bled.

This is what I had in my pockets

1. A Swiss Army Knife with 13 attachments including a wire-stripper and a saw and a toothpick and tweezers.

2. A piece of string.

3. A piece of a wooden puzzle which looked like this

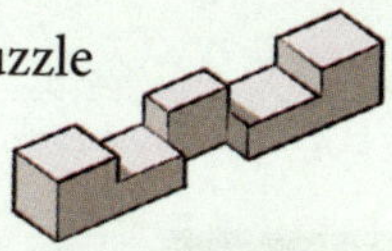

4. 3 pellets of rat food for Toby, my rat.

5. £1.47 (this was made up of a £1 coin, a 20p coin, two 10p coins, a 5p coin and a 2p coin).

6. A red paperclip.

7. A key for the front door.

I was also wearing my watch and they wanted me to leave this at the desk as well but I said that I needed to keep my watch on because I needed to know exactly what time it was. And when they tried to take it off me I screamed, so they let me keep it on.

They asked me if I had any family. I said I did. They asked me who my family was. I said it was Father, but Mother was dead. And I said it was also Uncle Terry but he was in Sunderland and he was Father's brother, and it was my grandparents, too, but three of them were dead and Grandma Burton was in a home because she had senile dementia and thought that I was someone on television.

Then they asked me for Father's phone number.

I told them that he had two numbers, one for at home and one which was a mobile phone and I said both of them.

It was nice in the police cell. It was almost a perfect cube, 2 metres long by 2 metres wide by 2 metres high. It contained approximately 8 cubic metres of air.

NOTE BOX

....
....
....
....
....
....
....
....
....
....
....
....
....
....
....
....
....

1 **Explain where the narrator is and why.**

....
....
....

2 **Tick what you can find in Christopher's pockets.**

3 **What do the contents of his pockets reveal about him?**

....

....

....

Joshua Jenkins as Christopher and Lucas Hare in 2018-2019 London theatre production of *The Curious Incident*.

4 **Complete Christopher's family tree.**

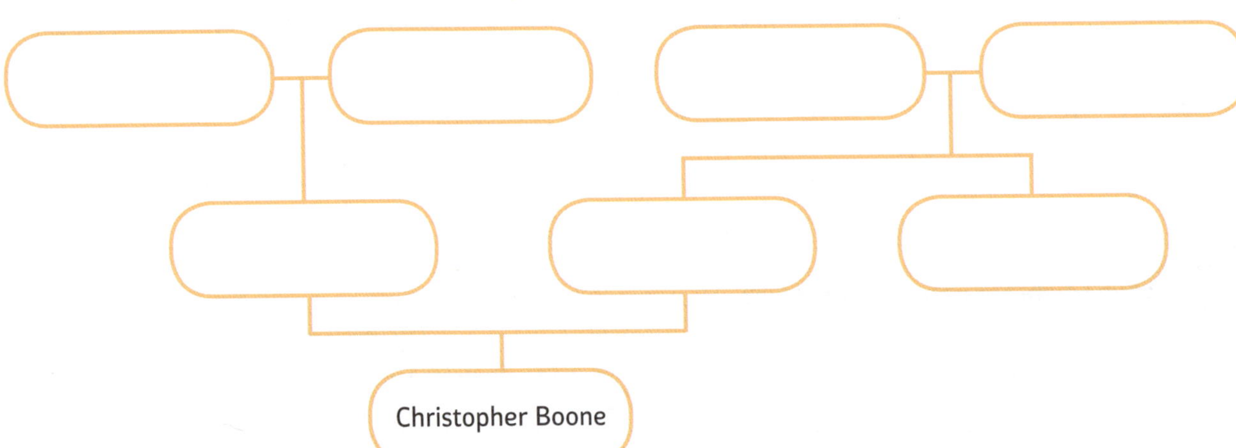

5 **Would you say that Christopher is:**

❒ claustrophobic ❒ hypersensitive ❒ cynical ❒ frightened ❒ precise ❒ cooperative

FOCUS ON... Lists

In literature **lists** are often associated with **verisimilitude** (see page 37). The reader has the impression that the narrator is reliable as he gives precise details. Actually, this is what is called an **effect of reality**.

● **Would you say that Christopher is a reliable or an unreliable narrator?**

....

....

....

SOUND LAB

<i>, <y> or <ee>

MP3

a **Listen to the words and write them in the correct column.**

paperclip • string • **k**ey • Swiss • kn**i**fe • toothpick • tw**ee**zers • Tob**y** • p**ie**ce • t**i**me • n**ee**ded • empt**y** • b**i**tten • m**y**self

/ɪ/	/aɪ/	/iː/
....	....	....
....	....	....
....	....	....
....	....	....
....	....	....

b **Listen again and repeat them.**

6 **Check your understanding**

● **Tick the correct answer. Christopher ....**

a. ... likes being ❒ with lot of people ❒ alone

b. ... has ❒ a kitten ❒ a rodent

c. ... likes ❒ mathematics ❒ poetry

d. ... has ❒ a large family ❒ a small family

READ ON

Now read the end of the chapter and sum up what Christopher wonders.

Read Chapter 29 and note the new things you learn about Christopher.

Extract 4

I find people confusing.

This is for two main reasons.

The first main reason is that people do a lot of talking without using any words. Siobhan says that if you raise one eyebrow[1] it can mean lots of different things. It can mean "I want to do sex with you" and it can also mean "I think that what you just said was very stupid."

Siobhan also says that if you close your mouth and breathe out loudly through your nose it can mean that you are relaxed, or that you are bored, or that you are angry and it all depends on how much air comes out of your nose and how fast and what shape your mouth is when you do it and how you are sitting and what you said just before and hundreds of other things which are too complicated to work out in a few seconds.

The second main reason is that people often talk using metaphors. These are examples of metaphors:

I laughed my socks off.

He was the apple of her eye.

They had a skeleton in the cupboard.

We had a real pig of a day.

The dog was stone dead.

The word metaphor means carrying something from one place to another, and it comes from the Greek words μετά (which means from one place to another) and φέρειν (which means to carry) and it is when you describe something by using a word for something that it isn't. This means that the word metaphor is a metaphor.

I think it should be called a lie because a pig is not like a day and people do not have skeletons in their cupboards. And when I try and make a picture of the phrase in my head it just confuses me because imagining an apple in someone's eye doesn't have anything to do with liking someone a lot and it makes you forget what the person was talking about.

My name is a metaphor. It means carrying Christ and it comes from the Greek words Χριστός (which means Jesus Christ) and φέρειν and it was the name given to St Christopher because he carried Jesus Christ across a river.

This makes you wonder what he was called before he carried Christ across the river. But he wasn't called anything because this is an apocryphal story which means that it is a lie, too.

Mother used to say that it meant Christopher was a nice name because it was a story about being kind and helpful, but I do not want my name to mean a story about being kind and helpful. I want my name to mean me.

NOTE BOX

....

....

....

....

....

....

....

....

....

....

....

....

....

....

....

....

....

1. *sourcil*

1 **What is the meaning of a metaphor?**

....

....

2 **What does the narrator compare the metaphor with?**

....

3 **Does the narrator like his name? Explain.**

....

....

....

TRANSLATION LAB

Translating metaphors

a **Reread the five metaphors. Are they all translatable into French using the same image?**

....

b **Look at the translations of the metaphors by the translator Odile Démange:**

C'est une bonne pâte.

Il était la prunelle de ses yeux.

Avoir un squelette dans le placard.

Il fait un temps de chien.

Elle est à la fleur de l'âge.

Would you choose the same translations, or would you make different choices?

....

....

Translating "as easy as ABC" as "*simple comme bonjour*" is called an **equivalence**. Proverbs in English and French don't always use the same images.

c **Find the equivalence for the following proverbs:**

- A bird in the hand is worth two in the bush.

....

- You can't have your cake and eat it.

....

- You can't judge a book by its cover.

....

FOCUS ON... Digression

Digression (from Latin *digressio* which means "going away") is the act of leaving the main subject in a discourse. In *The Curious Incident*, some passages or chapters seem to be far from the main plot.

Digressions may be confusing but they are meaningful because they contain clues, important information for the rest of the story.

a **Focus on the phrase:** "My mother used to say..." (l. 40)

What information does the expression "used to" give us?

....

....

b **What topic tackled in this chapter might be crucial later on?**

....

....

4 Check your understanding

● **Circle the correct information about Christopher.**

a. He is 15 years and 3 months and 2 days / 13 years and 2 months and 5 days.

b. He lives with his mother / his father / his uncle.

c. He decides to write a diary / a murder mystery novel.

d. He has a dog / a rat named Toby.

e. He likes / dislikes prime numbers and wet grass.

f. He assaulted a police officer because he touched / shouted at him.

YOUR TASK

You use your mobile phone to record a short presentation of Christopher's personality, likes and dislikes.

STEP 1. Browse what you wrote about Christopher in the note boxes.
STEP 2. Structure your notes into three categories: family, personality, likes and dislikes.
STEP 3. Record your presentation.

Family

....

Personality

....

Likes and dislikes

....

READ ON

Now read until chapter 43. Find information about the relationship between Christopher and his father.

PART 2 Christopher and his father

Read this extract from Chapter 43.

Extract 1

Mother died 2 years ago.

I came home from school one day and no one answered the door, so I went and found the secret key that we keep under a flowerpot behind the kitchen door. I let myself into the house and carried on making the Airfix Sherman Tank model I was building.

An hour and a half later Father came home from work. He runs a business and he does heating maintenance[1] and boiler repair with a man called Rhodri who is his employee. He knocked on the door of my room and opened it and asked whether I had seen Mother.

I said that I hadn't seen her and he went downstairs and started making some phone calls. I did not hear what he said.

Then he came up to my room and said he had to go out for a while and he wasn't sure how long he would be. He said that if I needed anything I should call him on his mobile phone.

He was away for 2½ hours. When he came back I went downstairs. He was sitting in the kitchen staring out of the back window down the garden to the pond[2] and the corrugated iron fence and the top of the tower of the church on Manstead Street which looks like a castle because it is Norman.

Father said, "I'm afraid you won't be seeing your mother for a while."

He didn't look at me when he said this. He kept on looking through the window.

Usually people look at you when they're talking to you. I know that they're working out what I'm thinking, but I can't tell what they're thinking. It is like being in a room with a one-way mirror in a spy film. But this was nice, having Father speak to me but not look at me.

I said, "Why not?"

He waited for a very long time, then he said, "Your mother has had to go into hospital."

"Can we visit her?" I asked, because I like hospitals. I like the uniforms and the machines.

Father said, "No."

I said, "Why can't we?"

And he said, "She needs rest. She needs to be on her own."

I asked, "Is it a psychiatric hospital?'"

And Father said, "No. It's an ordinary hospital. She has a problem… a problem with her heart."

1. *entretien des systèmes de chauffage* 2. *étang*

1 Fill in the table with information from the text.

Father	Mother	Rhodri	Christopher
....	....	....	....
....	....	....	....

2 **What literary device is used in this extract?** ❐ a prolepsis (or flashforward) ❐ an analepsis (flashback) .

Justify: ....

....

3 **Comment on the father's attitude when he speaks to Christopher.**

....

....

4 **a. What may the sentence "She has a problem... a problem with her heart" mean?**

....

....

b. What literary device is it?

❐ an understatement (*litote*) ❐ an innuendo (*sous-entendu*)
❐ a double-entendre (*double sens*) ❐ a metaphor

5 **Is the narrator aware of his father's lie?**

....

FOCUS ON... Discrepancy

The novel often depicts **situations of misunderstanding** between the narrator and the other characters. There is some **discrepancy** between what he understands and what the others do, essentially because he does not have access to the implicit. That may lead to **dramatic irony**: a situation (especially in drama) when a character does not know what the readers know.

GRAMMAR LAB

Reported speech

a **The father's words are mainly reported by Christopher very precisely. Turn this passage into direct speech:**

He knocked on the door of my room and opened it and asked whether I had seen Mother.
I said that I hadn't seen her and he went downstairs and started making some phone calls. I did not hear what he said.
Then he came up to my room and said he had to go out for a while and he wasn't sure how long he would be. He said that if I needed anything I should call him on his mobile phone.

....

....

....

....

....

b **Comment on the choice of direct speech here:**

Father said, "I'm afraid you won't be seeing your mother for a while."

....

....

6 Check your understanding

● **Circle the correct information about Christopher.**

a. Christopher remembers what happened two weeks ago / two years ago.

b. Christopher's mother had heart disease / a mental disorder.

c. Christopher's father informs Christopher immediately about his mother / waits before informing him about his mother.

d. Christopher remembers every detail of that day / forgot the details about that day.

READ ON

Read on until Chapter 79 and the extract below. Find information about Christopher's investigation.

▶ **Read this passage from Chapter 79. When the narrator explains a situation, it is always logical. Highlight a passage in the text for each of these functions:**
a. example in blue **b.** concept in green **c.** definition in red **d.** cause in yellow

Extract 2

When I got home Father was sitting at the table in the kitchen and he had made my supper. He was wearing a lumberjack shirt[1]. The supper was baked beans and broccoli and two slices of ham and they were laid out on the plate so that they were not touching.

He said, "Where have you been?"

And I said, "I have been out." This is called a white lie. A white lie is not a lie at all. It is where you tell the truth but you do not tell all the truth. This means that everything you say is a white lie because when someone says, for example, "What do you want to do today?" You say, "I want to do painting with Mrs Peters," but you don't say "I want to have my lunch and I want to go to the toilet and I want to go home after school and I want to play with Toby and I want to have my supper and I want to play on my computer and I want to go to bed." And I said a white lie because I knew that Father didn't want me to be a detective.

Father said, "I have just had a phone call from Mrs Shears."

I started eating my baked beans and broccoli and two slices of ham.

Then Father asked, "What the hell were you doing poking around her garden?"

I said, "I was doing detective work trying to find out who killed Wellington."

Father replied, "How many times do I have to tell you, Christopher?"

The baked beans and the broccoli and the ham were cold but I didn't mind this. I eat very slowly so my food is nearly always cold.

Father said, "I told you to keep your nose out of other people's business."

I said, "I think Mr Shears probably killed Wellington."

Father didn't say anything.

I said, "He is my Prime Suspect. Because I think someone might have killed Wellington to make Mrs Shears sad. And a murder is usually committed by someone known…"

Father banged the table with his fist really hard so that the plates and his knife and fork jumped around and my ham jumped sideways so that it touched the broccoli so I couldn't eat the ham and the broccoli any more.

1. *chemise de bûcheron*

NOTE BOX

....

....

1 Why is the father angry? Imagine what he might want to hide?

....

....

....

2 Explain what food reveals about the narrator's feelings.

....

....

....

....

....

WORD LAB

Adjectives and adverbs

Christopher's report is very neutral, factual. He does not characterise the characters' acts or tones. Add the words from the list that could be used.

all of a sudden • angrily • sharply • annoyed

a Father said ...., "Where have you been?"

b He said ...., "I have just had a phone call from Mrs Shears."

c Father asked ...., "What the hell were you doing poking around her garden?"

d ...., Father didn't say anything.

FOCUS ON... Foreshadowing

In detective stories or whodunnits, the author gives **clues and hints** about what is to come in the story. This is **foreshadowing**.

- **Explain why there may be foreshadowing in this extract.**

....

....

....

....

3 Check your understanding

● You took notes about the relationship between Christopher and his father but your notes have been stained by coffee. Complete them.

Christopher has lived with his father since his mother …… …… years ago. He runs a modest …… with one …… called Rhodri. He does not appreciate when Christopher …… as he has surely something to ……

YOUR TASK

You have written an e-mail to Ed Boone to understand better his relationship with his son when Christopher was 15. He writes you an e-mail to give you his viewpoint.

STEP 1. Ed Boone reacts to the mail (surprise but pride for his son).
STEP 2. He describes his relationship with his son when Christopher was 15.
STEP 3. He comments on it, focusing on his love for Christopher.

From : ed.boone@email.com
To:

READ ON

Read the last part of Chapter 79. Why is Christopher's father angry? What does he make Christopher promise?

PART 3

Christopher's dream

Read Chapter 83 and pick out all the things Christopher likes and dislikes.

I think I would make a very good astronaut.

To be a good astronaut you have to be intelligent and I'm intelligent. You also have to understand how machines work and I'm good at understanding how machines work. You also have to be someone who would like being on their own in a tiny spacecraft thousands and thousands of miles away from the surface of the earth and not panic or get claustrophobia or homesick or insane. And I like little spaces, so long as there is no one else in them with me. Sometimes when I want to be on my own I get into the airing cupboard in the bathroom and slide in beside the boiler[1] and pull the door closed behind me and sit there and think for hours and it makes me feel very calm.

So I would have to be an astronaut on my own or have my own part of the spacecraft which no one else could come into.

And also there are no yellow things or brown things in a spacecraft so that would be OK, too.

And I would have to talk to other people from Mission Control, but we would do that through a radio-link up and a TV monitor so they wouldn't be like real people who are strangers, but it would be like playing a computer game.

Also I wouldn't be homesick at all because I'd be surrounded by lots of the things I like, which are machines and computers and outer space. And I would like to be able to look out of the little window in the spacecraft and know that there was no one else near me for thousands and thousands of miles which is what I sometimes pretend at night in the summer when I go and lie on the lawn and look up at the sky and I put my hands around the sides of my face so that I can't see the fence and the chimney and the washing line and I can pretend I'm in space.

And all I could see would be stars. And stars are the places where the molecules that life is made of were constructed billions of years ago. For example, all the iron in your blood which stops you being anaemic was made in a star.

And I would like it if I could take Toby with me into space, and that might be allowed because they sometimes do take animals into space for experiments, so if I could think of a good experiment you could do with a rat that didn't hurt the rat, I could make them let me take Toby.

But if they didn't let me I would still go because it would be a Dream Come True.

1. *chaudière*

NOTE BOX

....

....

....

1 **Explain why being an astronaut is a job that could fit Christopher.**

....

....

2 **Is this project realistic / unrealistic? Justify your point of view.**

....

....

3 **Comment on the role of this chapter in the whole novel.**

....

GRAMMAR LAB

Would

a **Focus on these sentences.**

"I **would** have to talk to other people from Mission Control, but we **would** do that through a radio-link up and a TV monitor." (l. 12-13)
"Also I **wouldn't** be homesick at all because I'**d** be surrounded by lots of the things I like." (l. 15)

What meaning does *would* give? Tick the right answer:

❒ characteristic behaviour ❒ hypothetical situation ❒ absolute necessity

b **Imagine three things that would happen to Christopher if he wanted to be a doctor.**

....

....

....

FOCUS ON... *Gattaca*

Gattaca, a 1997 science-fiction film by Andrew Niccol, depicts a future society driven by eugenics. Children are conceived through genetic selection to possess the best hereditary traits of their parents. The film centres on Vincent who was conceived naturally and struggles to overcome genetic discrimination and realise his dream of becoming an astronaut.

a **What is common to the two stories?**

....

b **What does the dream of becoming an astronaut mean?**

....

....

4 **Check your understanding**

	True	False
a. Christopher thinks that he is clever.	❒	❒
b. Christopher does not like tiny places.	❒	❒
c. Christopher does not like talking to people.	❒	❒
d. Christopher does not like computers.	❒	❒

YOUR TASK

You need to illustrate your article. You call the illustrator to give him/her the indication of a picture that would represent "Christopher's dream".

STEP 1. Browse the elements that you would like to see (situation, characters, objects, etc.).

STEP 2. You may draw a sketch to help you.

STEP 3. Give your phone call and express what you would like and expect.

READ ON

Now read on to Chapter 107 noting information about Christopher's investigation.

PART 4 The Hound of the Baskervilles

Read Chapter 107 focusing on *The Hound of The Baskervilles.*

The Hound of the Baskervilles is my favourite book.

In *The Hound of the Baskervilles*, Sherlock Holmes and Doctor Watson get a visit from the moors[1] in Devon. James Mortimer's friend, Sir Charles Baskerville, has died of a heart attack and James Mortimer thinks that he might have been scared to death. James Mortimer also has an ancient scroll[2] which describes the curse[3] of the Baskervilles.

On this scroll it says that Sir Charles Baskerville had an ancestor called Sir Hugo Baskerville who was a wild, profane and godless man. And he tried to do sex with a daughter of a yeoman[4], but she escaped and he chased her across the moor. And his friends, who were dare-devil roisterers[5], chased after him.

And when they found him, the daughter of the yeoman had died of exhaustion and fatigue. And they saw a great, black beast shaped like a hound, yet larger than any hound that ever mortal eye has rested on, and this hound was tearing the throat out of Sir Hugo Baskerville. And one of his friends died of fear that every night and the other two were broken men for the rest of their days.

James Mortimer thinks that the Hound of the Baskervilles might have scared Sir Charles to death and he is worried that his son and heir, Sir Henry Baskerville, will be in danger when he goes to the Hall in Devon.

So Sherlock Holmes sends Doctor Watson to Devon with Sir Henry Baskerville and James Mortimer. And Doctor Watson tries to work out who might have killed Sir Charles Baskerville. And Sherlock Holmes says he will stay in London, but he travels to Devon secretly and does investigations of his own.

And Sherlock Holmes finds out that Sir Charles was killed by a neighbour called Stapleton who is a butterfly collector and a distant relation of the Baskervilles. And Stapleton is poor, so he tries to kill Sir Henry Baskerville so that he will inherit the Hall.

In order to do this he has thought a huge dog from London and covered it in phosphorus to make it glow[6] in the dark and it was this dog which scared Sir Charles Baskerville to death. And Sherlock Holmes and Watson and Lestrade from Scotland Yard catch him. And Sherlock Holmes and Watson shoot the dog, which is one of the dogs which gets killed in the story, which is not nice because it's not the dog's fault. And Stapleton escapes into the Grimpen Miren which is part of the moor, and he dies because he is sucked into a bog[7].

There are some bits of the story I don't like. One bit is the ancient scroll because it is written in old language which is difficult to understand like this

Learn then from this story not the fear the fruits of the past, but rather to be circumspect in the future, that those foul passions whereby our family has suffered so grievously may not again be loosed to our undoing.

And sometimes Sir Arthur Conan Doyle (who is the author) describes people like this

There was something subtly wrong with the face, some coarseness[8] of expression, some hardness, perhaps of eye, some looseness of lip which marred[9] its perfect beauty.

And I don't know what *some hardness, perhaps of eye* means, but I'm not interested in faces.

But sometimes it is fun not knowing what the words mean because you can look them up in the dictionary, like *goyal* (which is a deep dip) or *tors* (which are hills or rocky heights).

I like *The Hound of the Baskervilles* because it is a detective story which means that there are clues and Red Herrings[10].

TRANSLATION LAB

Dictionary study

Christopher likes looking up words in the dictionary when he does not know what they mean. Browse your monolingual dictionary to find the definitions of these words, then translate them into French in this context.

1. ....
2. ....
3. ....
4. ....
5. ....
6. ....
7. ....
8. ....
9. ....
10. ....

1 **Explain why *The Hound of the Baskervilles* is Christopher's favourite book.**

....

....

2 **What are the common points and the differences between *The Hound of the Baskervilles* and *The Curious Incident of the Dog in the Night-Time*?**

	Common points	Differences
Subjects	....	....
Style	....	....

FOCUS ON... Mise en abyme

The Hound of the Baskervilles is an **embedded story** in *The Curious Incident of the Dog in the Night-Time* as Christopher tells us the whole story in the book. It is a **story within a story** or a **mise en abyme**.

● **What do you think the embedded story brings to the novel?**

....

....

3 **Check your understanding**

	True	False
a. Christopher likes *The Hound of the Baskervilles* even if there are difficult words.	❒	❒
b. Christopher refuses to tell us the end of the story.	❒	❒
c. *The Hound of the Baskervilles* is a fantastic story.	❒	❒
d. Christopher does not give any comments when he tells the story.	❒	❒

YOUR TASK

As a journalist, you want to encourage teenagers to read. In your article, you write that Christopher Boone's favourite novel when he was young was *The Hound of the Baskervilles*. You ask your readers to post videos about their favourite novels. Make a video about your favourite novel as an example.

STEP 1. Choose your favourite novel.

STEP 2. Prepare its summary, stressing on the key-moments.

STEP 3. Record your video, telling us about the story and explaining what you liked and disliked.

READ ON

Now read on to Chapter 149. Comment on the relationship between Christopher and his father.

PART 5 About Christopher's mother

Read this excerpt from Chapter 149 and take notes about Christopher's mother.

And when I was in my room I shut the door and I took out the envelope from underneath my mattress. I held the letter up to the light to see if I could detect what was inside the envelope but the paper of the envelope was too thick. I wondered whether I should open the envelope because it was something I had taken from Father's room. But then I reasoned that it was addressed to me so it belonged to me so it was OK to open it.

So I opened the envelope. Inside there was a letter. And this was what was written in the letter.

451c Chapter Road
Willesden
London NW2 5NG
0208 887 8907

Dear Christopher,

I'm sorry it's been such a very long time since I wrote my last letter to you. I've been very busy. I've got a new job working as a secretary for a factory that makes things out of steel[1]*. You'd like it a lot. The factory is full of huge machines that make the steel and cut it and bend it into whatever shapes they need. This week they're making a roof for a cafe in a shopping centre in Birmingham. It's shaped like a huge flower and they're going to stretch canvas over it to make it like an enormous tent.*

Also we've moved into the new flat at last as you can see from the address. It's not as nice as the old one and I don't like Willesden very much, but it's easier for Roger to get to work and he's bought it (he only rented the other one), so we can get our own furniture and paint the walls the colour we want to.

And that's why it's such a long time since I wrote my last letter to you because it's been hard work packing up all our things and then unpacking them and then getting used to this new job.

I'm very tired now and I must go to sleep and I want to put this into the letterbox tomorrow morning, so I'll sign off now and write you another letter soon.

You haven't written to me yet, so I know that you are probably still angry with me, I'm sorry Christopher. But I still love you. I hope you don't stay angry with me forever. And I'd love it if you were able to write me a letter (but remember to send it to the new address!)

I think about you all the time.

Lots of love,

Your Mum,

XXXXXX

Then I was really confused because Mother had never worked as a secretary for a firm that made things out of steel. Mother had worked as a secretary for a big garage in the centre of town. And Mother had never lived in London. Mother had always lived with us. And Mother had never written a letter to me before.

There was no date on the letter so I couldn't work out when Mother had written the letter and I wondered whether someone else had written the letter and pretended to be Mother.

And then I looked at the front of the envelope and I saw that there was a postmark and there was a date on the postmark and it was quite difficult to read, but it said

Which meant that the letter was posted on 16th October 1997, which was 18 months after Mother had died.

1. *acier*

NOTE BOX

....

....

1 **Why does the narrator hesitate to open the envelope?**

....

2 **What information does the letter bring?**

Mother's new life	Mother's feelings	Father's acts
....	....	....
....	....	....
....	....	....

3 **To you is the murder of the dog the main plot of *The Curious Incident of the Dog in the Night-Time*?**

....

4 **What does this revelation mean about the plot of the novel?**

....

TRANSLATION LAB

Adverbs of time

a **Observe the sentence:**

You haven't written to me ***yet****, so I know that you are probably* ***still*** *angry with me.*

- Which words refer to an action or state that started in the past and continues to the present?

....

- What word is used with an affirmative statement? Where is the word in the sentence?

....

- What word is used with a negative statement? Where is the word in the sentence?

....

b **Translate the following sentences into English.**

- *Christopher n'a pas encore trouvé le meurtrier.*

....

- *Il n'en croit pas ses yeux. Il est encore en train de lire la lettre.*

....

FOCUS ON... The plot twist

A **plot twist** introduces a radical change in the direction or expected outcome of the plot.

a Where is the plot twist situated in *The Curious Incident*?

....

b What does it mean about the novel?

....

....

c Who is the detective?

....

d What is the mystery?

....

....

5 Check your understanding

● **This is a summary of the passage. Find 6 mistakes and correct them.**

Christopher found an envelope in his father's bedside table and opened it immediately. The letter comes from Christopher's mother. She now lives alone in Newcastle. She works as an accountant for a steel factory. She says she would like to receive a letter from her son. Christopher's first reaction was joy.

YOUR TASK

You are astonished by what you have read. Immediately, you write an e-mail to your editor-in-chief to tell him/her what you have learnt about Christopher's childhood.

STEP 1. You sum up the contents of the letter you have read.
STEP 2. You explain to your editor-in-chief what happened to Christopher.
STEP 3. You react to the situation.

From : .... @sciencefocus.co.uk
To:

....

....

....

....

READ ON

Now read on to the extract from chapter 167 on the next page. Focus on the letters. What do they say about Christopher's mother?

PART 6

The revelation

Read this excerpt from chapter 167 and take notes about what Christopher's father says.

I sat on the bed and looked at my knees.

So Father went out of the room and picked up my clothes from the bathroom floor and put them on the landing. Then he went and got the sheets from his bed and brought them out onto the landing together with my shirt and my jumper. Then he picked them all up and took them downstairs. Then I heard him start the washing machine and I heard the boiler starting up and the water in the water pipes going into the washing machine.

That was all I could hear for a long time.

I doubled 2s in my head because it made me feel calmer. I got to **33,554,432** which is $\mathbf{2^{25}}$, which is not very much because I've got to $\mathbf{2^{45}}$ before, but my brain wasn't working very well.

Then Father came back into the room again and said, "How are you feeling? Can I get you anything?"

I didn't say anything. I carried on looking at my knees.

And Father didn't say anything either. He just sat down on the bed next to me and put his elbows on his knees and looked down at the carpet between his legs where there was a little red piece of Lego with eight nobbles on.

Then I heard Toby waking up, because he is nocturnal, and I heard him rustling in his cage.

And Father was silent for a really long time.

Then he said, "Look, maybe I shouldn't say this, but... I want you to know that you can trust me. And... OK, maybe I don't tell the truth all the time. God knows, I try, Christopher. God knows I do, but... Life is difficult, you know. It's bloody hard telling the truth all the time. Sometimes it's impossible. And I want you to know that I'm trying, I really am. And perhaps this is not a very good time to say this, and I know you're not going to like it, but... you have to know that I am going to tell you the truth from now on. About everything. Because... If you don't tell the truth now, then later on...later on it hurts even more. So..."

Father rubbed his face with his hands and pulled his chin down with his fingers and stared at the wall, I could see him out of the corner of my eye.

And he said, "I killed Wellington, Christopher."

I wondered if this was a joke, because I don't understand jokes, and when people tell jokes they don't mean what they say.

But then Father said, "Please, Christopher. Just...let me explain." Then he sucked in some air and he said, "When your mum left... Eileen... Mrs Shears... she was very good to us. Very good to me. She helped me through a very difficult time. And I'm not sure I would have made it without her. Well, you know how she was round here most days. Helping out with the cooking and the cleaning. Popping over to see if we were OK, if we needed anything... I thought... Well... Shit, Christopher, I'm trying to keep this simple... I thought she might carry on coming over. I thought... and maybe I was being stupid... I thought she might... eventually... want to move in[1] here. Or that we might move into her house. We... we got on really, really well. I thought we were friends. And I guess[2] I thought wrong. I guess... in the end... it comes down to... shit... we argued, Christopher, and... She said some things I'm not going to say to you because they're not nice, but they hurt, but... I think she cared more for that bloody dog than for me, for us. And maybe that's not so stupid, looking back. Maybe we are a bloody handful[3]. And maybe it is easier living on your own looking after some stupid mutt, than sharing your life with other

... / ...

1. come to live 2. suppose, imagine 3. difficult

actual human beings. I mean, shit, buddy, we're not exactly low-maintenance[4], are we…? Anyway, we had this row[5]. Well, quite a few rows to be honest. But after this particularly nasty little blow-out, she chucked me out[6] of the house. And you know what that bloody dog was like after the operation. Bloody schizophrenic. Nice as pie one moment, roll over, tickle its stomach. Sink its teeth[7] into your leg the next. Anyway, we're yelling at each other and it's in the garden relieving itself[8]. So when she slams the door behind me the bugger's waiting for me. And… I know, I know. Maybe if I'd just given it a kick it would probably have backed off. But, shit, Christopher, when that red mist comes down[9]… Christ, you know how it is. I mean, we're not that different, me and you. And all I could think was that she cared more about this bloody dog than she did about you or me. And it was like everything I'd been bottling up[10] for two years just…"

Then Father was silent for a bit.

Then he said, "I'm sorry, Christopher. I promise you. I never meant for it to turn out like this."

And then I knew that it wasn't a joke and I was really frightened.

4. easy to care for, requiring little work 5. argument 6. throw out 7. bite, attack with the teeth 8. urinate 9. anger causes you to see red 10. keep inside, repress

NOTE BOX

....

....

1 Explain what the father reveals and his reasons.

....

....

....

2 Describe the narrator's feelings and how they are conveyed.

....

....

....

3 Focus on the narrative technique and show how tension is built up. These guidelines are here to help you:

a. Who speaks?

....

b. How? (use of pronouns, voice flow)

....

....

....

4 Pick out the climactic sentence:

....

5 Account for the role of silent moments in the scene.

....

....

FOCUS ON... The monologue vs the soliloquy

In drama, a monologue is a long speech during a conversation while a soliloquy is when a character makes a speech alone, revealing his or her thoughts.

- **Is the father's speech a monologue or a soliloquy? Explain.**

....

....

....

STYLE LAB

Peripeteia and anagnorisis (Aristotle)

Peripeteia is the reversal from one state to its opposite. Some element in the plot effects a reversal, so that the hero who thought he was in good shape suddenly finds that all is lost, or vice versa. **Anagnorisis** is a change from ignorance to knowledge, a revelation.

- **Does this excerpt feature a peripeteia or an anagnorisis? Explain.**

....

....

SOUND LAB

Intonation and pauses

MP3

Listen to the passage from l. 31, "Well, you," to l. 39, "for us", focusing on intonation and pauses. Practise saying it as if you were Christopher's father.

6 Check your understanding

- **Say if each statement is true or false and justify your answer.**

	True	False
a. Eileen Shears was Ed Boone's lover.	❐	❐
b. Ed Boone proposed to Eileen.	❐	❐
c. Ed Boone killed Wellington because of jealousy.	❐	❐
d. Christopher forgives his father.	❐	❐

YOUR TASK

You are struck by this passage. You meet your editor-in-chief to tell him/her what you have learnt. You read the father's speech loud to inform him/her about what you know. Make it sound real.

STEP 1. You sum up the situation.

STEP 2. You react to what happened.

STEP 3. You read a passage from the novel, pretending to be the father.

READ ON

Read on to the next extract, from Chapter 191, focusing on Christopher's plans. What has changed for him?

PART 7

The runaway

Read this extract from Chapter 191 and focus on Christopher's situation.

Extract 1

And then I looked up and saw that there was a policeman standing in front of me and was saying, "Anyone at home?" but I didn't know what that meant.

And then he said, "Are you all right, young man?"

I looked at him and I thought for a bit so that I would answer the question correctly and I said, "No."

And he said, "You're looking a bit worse for wear."

He had a gold ring on one of his fingers and it had curly letters on it but I couldn't see what the letters were.

Then he said, "The lady at the café says you've been here to 2½ hours and when she tried talking to you, you were in a complete trance."

Then he said, "What's your name?"

And I said, "Christopher Boone."

And he said, "Where do you live?"

And I said, "36 Randolph Street" and I started feeling better because I like policemen and it was an easy question, and I wondered whether I should tell him that Father killed Wellington and whether he would arrest Father.

And he said, "What are you doing here?"

And I said, "I needed to sit down and be quiet and think."

And he said, "OK, let's keep it simple. What are you doing at the railway station?"

And I said, "I'm going to see Mother."

And he said, "Mother?"

And I said, "Yes, Mother."

And he said, "When's your train?"

And I said, "I don't know. She lives in London. I don't know when there's a train to London."

And he said, "So you don't live with your mother?"

And I said, "No. But I'm going to."

NOTE BOX

1 Identify the characters and the situation.

2 **What does Christopher intend to do? Explain why.**

....

....

....

....

3 **Observe the beginning of sentences. What can you notice about the style and the level of English. What does it reflect?**

....

....

....

....

FOCUS ON... **Verisimilitude**

Verisimilitude is the appearance of being true or real.

● **Explain how Haddon achieves verisimilitude in the way Christopher writes.**

....

....

....

TRANSLATION LAB

Initiation aux techniques de traduction

a **Observe les passages ci-dessous et leur traduction.**

1. And I said, "I needed to sit down and be quiet and think."	*J'ai dit: « il fallait que je reste assis au calme, pour réfléchir. »*	....
2. And he said, "OK, let's keep it simple."	*Il a dit: « Bien, procédons dans l'ordre. »*	....
3. "What are you doing at the railway station?"	*« Qu'est-ce que tu fais à la gare? »*	....

● **Parmi les procédés de traduction, il y a:**

i. *la traduction littérale, ou mot à mot ;*

ii. *la transposition d'une catégorie grammaticale à une autre ;*

iii. *l'équivalence: traduction grâce à une rédaction différente.*

● **Associez les exemples avec les procédés de traduction utilisés dans le tableau.**

b **Traduisez la fin de l'extrait depuis *And he said, "When's your train?"* (l. 26).**

....

....

....

....

....

....

4 **Look at *The Runaway* by Norman Rockwell, and find the similarities and the differences between this passage and Rockwell's illustration.**

Site

....

....

....

5 Check your understanding

● **Tick true or false and justify you answers.**

	True	False
a. Christopher is sitting at the railway station.	❐	❐
....		
b. He has been waiting for his father for hours.	❐	❐
....		
c. A lady was worried about his situation.	❐	❐
....		
d. Christopher is lost.	❐	❐
....		

READ ON

Now read on to Chapter 227 and the extract below, focusing on Christopher's reactions during the trip.

▶ **Read this extract from chapter 227 and focus on what happens to Christopher.**

Extract 2

And the train came into the little station and it stopped and 5 people got into the train and another person ran into the little station and got on, and 7 people got off the train and then the doors closed automatically and the train went away. And when the next train came I wasn't so scared any more because the sign said TRAIN APPROACHING so I knew it was going to happen.

And then I decided that I would look for Toby because there were only 3 people in the little station. So I stood up and I looked up and down the little station and in the doorways that went into tunnels but I couldn't see him anywhere. And then I looked down into the black, lower-down bit where the rails were.

And then I saw two mice and they were black because they were covered in dirt. And I liked that because I like mice and rats. But they weren't Toby. So I carried on looking.

And then I saw Toby, and he was also in the lower-down bit where the rails were, and I knew he was Toby because he was white and he had a brown egg shape on his back. So I climbed down off the concrete[1]. And he was eating a bit of rubbish that was an old sweet paper. And someone shouted. "Jesus. What are you doing?"

And I bent down to catch Toby but he ran off. And I walked after him and I bent down again and I said, "Toby… Toby… Toby…" and I held out my hand so that I could smell my hand and smell that it was me.

And someone said, "Get out of there, for fuck's sake." And I looked up and it was a man who was wearing a green raincoat and he had black shoes and his socks were showing and they were grey with little diamond patterns on them.

And I said, '"Toby… Toby…" but he ran off again.

1. *béton*

And the man with the diamond patterns on his socks tried to grab[2] my shoulder, so I screamed. And then I heard the sound like swordfighting[3] and Toby started running again, but this time he ran the other way, which was past my feet and I grabbed at him and I caught him by the tail.

And the man with the diamond patterns on his socks said, "Oh Christ. Oh Christ."

And then I heard the roaring and I lifted Toby up and grabbed him with both hands and he bit me on my thumb and there was blood coming out and I shouted and Toby tried to jump out of my hands.

And then the roaring got louder and I turned round and I saw the train coming out of the tunnel and I was going to be run over and killed so I tried to climb up onto the concrete but it was high and I was holding Toby in both my hands.

And then the man with the diamond patterns on his socks grabbed hold of me and pulled me and I screamed, but he kept pulling me and he pulled me onto the concrete and we fell over and I carried on screaming because he had hurt my shoulder. And then the train came into the station and I stood up and I ran to the bench again and I put Toby into the pocket inside my jacket and he went very quiet and he didn't move.

And the man with the diamond patterns on his socks was standing next to me and he said, "What the fuck do you think you were playing at?"

But I didn't say anything.

NOTE BOX

....

2. *saisir* 3. *combat à l'épée*

1 Where is the narrator and what happens to him?

....

....

....

2 Why is this episode a real challenge for him?

....

....

....

3 What does the presence of 'the man with the diamond patterns on his socks' bring?

....

....

....

4 **Why is 'Train approaching' written differently in the text?**

....

5 **Observe the beginning of the sentences in this passage.**

a. What words does Christopher use? ....

b. What effect does the use of these linkwords give?

....

....

6 **What makes this extract full of suspense and trepidation?**

....

....

....

FOCUS ON... Coming-of-age stories

A coming-of-age story is a genre of literature that focuses on the growth of a protagonist from youth to adulthood.

There are many famous coming of age stories: *Little Women* by Louisa May Alcott, *The Catcher in the Rye* by J.D. Salinger, *Jane Eyre* by Charlotte Brontë, *To Kill a Mockingbird* by Harper Lee, *Huckleberry Finn* by Mark Twain, etc.

● **Explain why we could say that *The Curious Incident* is a coming-of-age story.**

....

....

Emma Watson, Florence Pugh, Saoirse Ronan and Eliza Scanlen as the March sisters in Greta Gerwig's 2019 film adaptation of *Little Women*.

WORD LAB

Senses and movement

● **Highlight the verbs (in yellow) and the nouns (in green) in the text linked to senses and movement and classify them into the right column:**

Sound	Sight	Touch	Movement
....	....	....	....
....	....	....	....
....	....	....	....
....	....	....	....

7 Check your understanding

● Put the events into the right chronological order:

_______ The man with the diamond patterns on his socks helps Christopher.

_______ Toby bites Christopher.

_______ Toby runs off.

_______ Toby escapes again.

_______ Christopher waits in the Underground.

_______ The man shouts at Christopher angrily.

_______ The train enters the station.

The Underground scene from the 2018-2019 London theatre production of *The Curious Incident of the Dog in the Night-Time.*

YOUR TASK

You have found the policeman or "the man with the diamond patterns on his socks", who tells you the story from his point of view. Write up the interview for your article.

STEP 1. Choose the character you want to interview.

STEP 2. Think of the questions that are relevant to know more about Christopher's personality.

STEP 3. Give the character's answers.

READ ON

Carry on reading Chapter 227 until the extract on the next page, focusing on Christopher.

PART 8

Reunions

Read this second excerpt from chapter 227 and find information about Christopher's mother's situation.

Extract 1

And then it was 11:32 p.m. and I heard voices of people walking along the street.

And a voice said, "I don't care whether you thought it was funny or not," and it was a lady's voice.

And another voice said, "Judy, look. I'm sorry, OK," and it was a man's voice.

And the other voice, which was the lady's voice, said. "Well, perhaps you should have thought about that before you made me look like a complete idiot."

And the lady's voice was Mother's voice.

And mother came into the garden and Mr Shears was with her and the other voice was his.

So I stood up and I said, "You weren't in, so I waited for you."

And Mother said, "Christopher."

And Mr Shears said, "What?"

And Mother put her arms around me and said, "Christopher, Christopher, Christopher."

And I pushed her away because she was grabbing me and I didn't like it, and I pushed really hard and I fell over.

And Mr Shears said, "What the hell is going on?"

And Mother said, "I'm so sorry, Christopher. I forgot."

And I was lying on the ground and Mother held up her right hand and spread her fingers out in a fan so that I could touch her fingers, but then I saw that Toby had escaped out of my pocket so I had to catch him.

And Mr Shears said, "I suppose this means Ed's here."

And there was a wall around the garden so Toby couldn't get out because he was stuck in the corner and he couldn't climb up the walls fast enough and I grabbed him and put him back in my pocket and I said, "He's hungry. Have you got any food I can give him and some water?"

And Mother said, "Where's your father, Christopher?"

And I said, "I think he's in Swindon.""

And Mr Shears said, "Thank God for that."

And Mother said, "But how did you get here?"

And my teeth were clicking against each other because of the cold and I couldn't stop them, and I said, "I came on the train. And it was really frightening. And I took Father's cashpoint card so I could get money out and a policeman helped me. But then he wanted to take me back to Father. And he was on the train with me. But then he wasn't."

And Mother said, "Christopher, you're soaking[1]. Roger, don't just stand there."

And then she said, "Oh my God. Christopher. I didn't...I didn't think I'd ever...Why are you here on your own?"

And Mr Shears said, "Are you going to come in or are you going to stay out here all night?"

And I said, "I'm going to live with you because Father killed Wellington with a garden fork and I'm frightened of him."

And Mr Shears said, "Jumping Jack Christ."

1. *tout mouillé*

NOTE BOX

....

....

....

1 **Describe the situation (characters, time, setting).**

....

....

2 **Identify the different characters' preoccupations.**

Christopher	The mother	Roger
....	....	....
....	....	....
....	....	....

3 **Analyse this reunion. Is it emotional as it should be?**

....

....

4 **Comment on Roger's last question and Christopher's answer. What effect does this dialogue provoke?**

....

....

SOUND LAB

The intonation of questions

a **Listen to the following questions. Is the tone rising ↑ or falling ↓?** MP3

1. What the hell is going on? ....

2. Where's your father, Christopher? ....

3. But how did you get here? ....

4. Have you got any food I can give him and some water? ....

5. Are you going to come in or are you going to stay out here all night? ....

- **What can you deduce about the intonation of questions?**

....

b **Repeat them with the correct tone.**

FOCUS ON... Humour

In literature there are many devices that create humour: slapstick (embarrassing situation), incongruity, play-on-words, surprise, irony, or exaggeration.

● **Among these devices, can you spot one or two that are used in this extract?**

....

5 Check your understanding

● **Tick true or false.**

	True	False
a. Christopher throws himself into his mother's arms.	❒	❒
b. Christopher is aggressive because his mother lied to him.	❒	❒
c. Roger is worried about Christopher's coming.	❒	❒
d. Christopher is no longer concerned with Toby.	❒	❒

READ ON

Carry on reading till the final chapter, 233, and the extract below. What happens to Christopher's mother and Roger?

▶ **Read this excerpt from Chapter 233 and focus on the relationship between Christopher and his father.**

Extract 2

Father said, "Christopher, look… Things can't go on like this. I don't know about you, but this… this just hurts too much. You being in the house but refusing to talk to me… You have to learn to trust me… And I don't care how long it takes… If it's a minute one day and two minutes the next and three minutes the next and it takes years I don't care. Because this is important. This is more important than anything else."

And then he tore a little strip of skin[1] away from the side of the thumbnail on his left hand.

And then he said, "Let's call it… let's call it a project. A project we have to do together. You have to spend more time with me. And I… I have to show you that you can trust me. And it will be difficult at first because… because it's a difficult project. But it will get better. I promise."

Then he rubbed the sides of his forehead with his fingertips, and he said, "You don't have to say anything, not right now. You just have to think about it. And, um… I've got you a present. To show you that I really mean what I say. And to say sorry. And because… well, you'll see what I mean."

Then he got out of the armchair and he walked over to the kitchen door and opened it and there was a big cardboard box on the floor and there was a blanket in it and he bent down and put his hands inside the box and he took a little sandy-coloured dog out.

Then he came back through and gave me the dog. And he said, "He's two months old. And he's a Golden Retriever."

And the dog sat in my lap and I stroked it.

And no one said anything for a while.

Then Father said, "Christopher. I would never, ever do anything to hurt you."

Then no one said anything.

Then Mother came into the room and said, "You won't be able to take him away with you, I'm afraid. The bedsit[2]'s too small. But your Father's going to look after him here. And you can come and take him out for walks whenever you want."

And I said, "Does he have a name?"

1. *peau* 2. very small flat with just one room

NOTE BOX

1 **What does Christopher's father try to do and why?**

2 **When does Christopher speak? What does it mean?**

3 **To what extent is the gift symbolic?**

TRANSLATION LAB

Possessives

a **Look at these sentences and their translations:**

a. Then he rubbed the sides of **his** forehead with **his** fingertips.	*Puis il se frotta* ***les*** *tempes avec* ***le*** *bout des doigts.*
b. He bent down and put **his** hands inside the box.	*Il se pencha et mis* ***les*** *mains dans la boîte.*

- **What do you notice?**

b **Translate these sentences:**

He washed his hands.

She combed her hair.

She got a flower tattoo on her shoulder.

Stuart Laing as Ed and Joshua Jenkins as Christopher in *The Curious Incident of the Dog in the Night-Time*, London 2018-2019.

FOCUS ON... Conflicts and reconciliation

a There are many **conflicts** in *The Curious Incident*:

– person vs person ....

– person vs self ....

– person vs society ....

● **Can you find an example for any of these entries?**

b So the denouement is a **reconciliation**.

● **Why does this reconciliation surpass the father-son reconciliation?**

....

....

4 Check your understanding

● **Tick true or false.**

	True	False
a. Christopher refuses to speak to his father as he lied to him.	❒	❒
b. The father gives Christopher a dog to reopen dialogue.	❒	❒
c. Christopher first refuses the dog as it is yellow.	❒	❒
d. The father and the mother live together again.	❒	❒

READ ON

Now read on to the final extract, the book's ending, focusing on the message of the novel.

Read the ending of the book, the last part of chapter 233 and take notes about Christopher's evolution.

Extract 3

And I called the dog Sandy. And Father bought him a collar and a lead and I was allowed to take him for walks to the shop and back. And I played with him with a rubber bone.

And Mother got flu[1] and I had to spend three days with Father and stay in his house. But it was OK because Sandy slept on my bed so he would bark if anyone came into the room during the night. And Father made a vegetable patch in the garden and I helped him. And we planted carrots and peas and spinach and I'm going to pick them and eat them when they're ready.

And I went to a bookshop with Mother and I bought a book called *Further Maths for A Level* and Father told Mrs Gascoyne that I was going to take A Level Further Maths next year and she said, "OK."

And I am going to pass it and get an A grade. And in two years' time I am going to take A Level Physics and get an A grade.

And then, when I've done that, I am going to go to university in another town. And it doesn't have to be in London because I don't like London and there are universities in lots of places and not all of them are in big cities. And I can live in a flat with a garden and a proper toilet. And I can take Sandy and my books and my computer.

And then I will get a First Class Honours Degree[2] and I will become a scientist.

And I know I can do this because I went to London on my own, and because I solved the mystery of Who killed Wellington? and I found my mother and I was brave and I wrote a book and that means I can do anything.

NOTE BOX

1. *la grippe* 2. the top level of undergraduate degree

1 **Say why the end of the novel corresponds to the saying: "All is well that ends well."**

2 **To what extent can the narrator be a role model?**

GRAMMAR LAB

The future

a Observe the two sentences.

1. *And I am going to pass it and get an A grade. And in two years' time I am going to take A level Physics and get an A grade.*
2. *And then I will get a First Class Honours Degree and I will become a scientist.*

- **Which sentence corresponds to:**

An intention, a project: _______

The speaker's involvement: _______

b What shows that Christopher is confident and determined?

....

....

3 Check your understanding

- **These three sentences are incomplete. Finish them.**

a. Father managed to reconcile with Christopher thanks to ....

....

b. As Christopher is very good at maths, he ....

....

c. Christopher gained confidence because ....

....

YOUR TASK

Now, you have finished the book. You have all the elements to write your article about Christopher Boone.

STEP 1. Focus on this book showing how it has enabled him to become the man he is.
STEP 2. Show how he can be a role model for everyone.
STEP 3. Write the article. Don't forget the headline, the subheading and a picture.

....

....

....

....

....

....

....

....

EXIT TEST

Exit test 1

Fill in the blanks to make a summary of *The Curious Incident of the Dog in the Night-Time*. You can use the word cloud below to help you.

annoys changes apologises confiscates
behavioural
carries on argument difficult
killed fifteen father runs away dog
fork investigate forbids
solved lied letters
scientist live trust left London
Mrs Shears mother maths
succeed in novel Sandy
wrote passes
reconciles rat teenager
two

Christopher Boone is a (1) ______________ year-old boy who describes himself as a (2) ______________ with some (3) ______________ difficulties. He has lived with his (4) ______________ since his (5) ______________ died (6) ______________ years ago.

One night, Christopher finds a dog lying on the grass with a (7) ______________ sticking out of it. The dog, Wellington, is dead. He belonged to (8) ______________. Christopher decides to (9) ______________ who killed Wellington and write a (10) ______________ about this.

The investigation (11) ______________ his father, who (12) ______________ him from continuing. But, Christopher (13) ______________ and his father (14) ______________ the book. When Christopher looks for it, he discovers some (15) ______________ in his father's bedroom. They come from his (16) ______________, who (17) ______________ the family to (18) ______________ with Roger Shears. Christopher's father thus reveals that he (19) ______________ to his son to protect him and (20) ______________ for that. He then adds that he had an affair with (21) ______________ and while he was having an (22) ______________ with her, Wellington came after him and he killed the dog.

Christopher does not (23) ______________ his father anymore and decides to go to (24) ______________ with his pet (25) ______________ Toby to live with his mother. The journey is (26) ______________ as Toby (27) ______________ and he is almost (28) ______________ by a Tube train.

He finally arrives at his (29) ______________'s and tells her that he wants to live with her, which (30) ______________ her relationship with Roger Shears. At the end, Christopher (31) ______________ his A-level in (32) ______________. He (33) ______________ with his father, as he gives him a (34) ______________ called (35) ______________.

As a conclusion, Christopher says that he will (36) ______________ everything (his plan is to become a (37) ______________) as he (38) ______________ a mystery, went to (39) ______________ alone and (40) ______________ a book.

EXIT TEST

Exit test 2

QUIZ

1. Complete the blanks with the letters of the key moments of the novel. Then match the key moments with the narrative stages they correspond to.

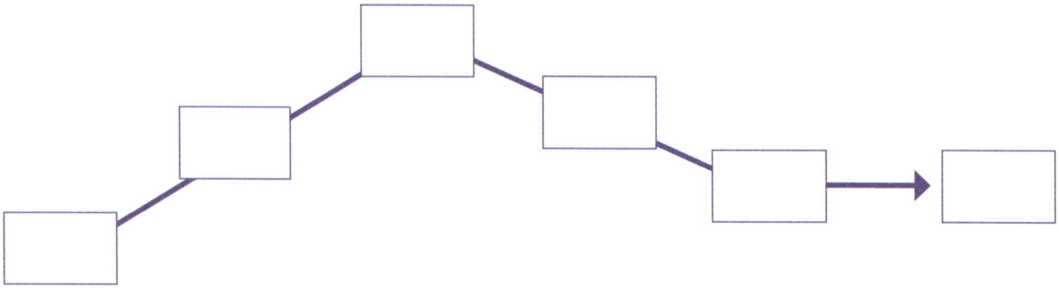

a. The discovery of the dog. ●	● **i.** scene of exposition
b. Christopher runs away. ●	● **ii.** falling action
c. Christopher finds his mother. ●	● **iii.** climax
d. Reconciliation. ●	● **iv.** epilogue
e. The investigation. ●	● **v.** denouement
f. Christopher learns all the truth. ●	● **vi.** rising action

2. Who said what?

Father • Mother • Mr Shears • Mrs Shears • Siobhan • Christopher

a. "You should write something you would want to read yourself." ....

b. "I'm going to get an A grade. And that's why I have to go back to Swindon." ....

c. "Are you going to come in or are you going to stay out here all night?" ....

e. "Why didn't you write to me, Christopher?" ....

d. "She has a problem...a problem with her heart." ....

f. "Let go of the dog!" ....

3. What genre is *The Curious Incident of the Dog in The Night-Time*? a whodunnit? a coming-of-age novel? a play? an adventure novel? Justify your point of view.

....

....

4. Give a definition of these expressions:

a. white lie: ....

b. a joke: ....

c. a metaphor: ....

d. What do they have in common for Christopher? ....

....

5. a. What colours does Christopher like? What colours does he dislike?

....

b. What does the name of the dog "Sandy" reveal at the end?

....

6. To what extent is *The Curious Incident of the Dog in the Night-Time* a novel about logic?

....

7. a. Whose point of view is given throughout the novel?

....

b. Would you say that the narrator is reliable/unreliable? Justify. ....

....

8. Who was misled throughout the novel? Explain. ....

....

9. How does the novel play with emotions? Is it lack of emotions? Full of emotions? Explain.

....

....

10. Explain the title. ....

....

AROUND THE BOOK

FROM BOOK TO PLAY

Simon Stephens's award-winning theatre adaptation of *The Curious Incident of the Dog in the Night-Time* opened in London in 2012 and has had a Broadway run in New York and a popular international tour.

1 Look at the still. What scene does it correspond to? Explain.

2 Dramatisation: Remember the elements in the book that are related to drama. Note them down.

3 To you, is *The Curious Incident of The Dog in the Night-Time* a suitable book for a theatre adaptation? Explain.

> **GOING FURTHER** Video
>
> Dr Temple Grandin is an American scientist with autism. In this video, she discusses how her brain (or as she calls it, her search engine) works.

4 Creativity: Watch the trailer. Pick out the original elements that the show permits in comparison to the book. Video

5 Would you like to watch the show? What appeals / does not appeal to you about the trailer?

FROM PAGE TO STAGE

Watch Mark Haddon and playwright Simon Stephens discussing how Stephens adapted an "unadaptable" novel for the stage.

Video

1 **Listen to Mark Haddon. What was his opinion about the possibility of a stage or film adaptation?**

2 **Imagine Simon Stephens's reasons for thinking the book is adaptable. For example, is the scene in the photo something that Christopher does?**

FROM BOOK TO FILM

Kia and Cosmos is a Bengali film freely adapted from *The Curious Incident of the Dog in the Night-Time*. It was directed by Sudipto Roy (2018). It is set in Kolkata, India.

Kia Chatterjee is a special girl with special needs. She has just hit her teens; she has an incredibly sharp mind and a photographic memory. Her favourite pastimes are rattling off prime and Fibonacci numbers to herself, counting red cars on the streets and writing her diary. Kia lives with her mother; her father has succumbed to cardiac problems. She has fond memories of her father, though. And although it may seem that she is incapable of feeling grief, she is devastated by her father's untimely departure. When her pet cat Cosmos dies a few weeks pregnant, Kia's sixth sense tells her that the poor animal's death was anything but natural, and that she was murdered. She vows to find the culprit and embarks upon a journey that will lead her to a shocking truth.

Bhaskar Chattopadhyay, Firstpost.com, 2019

Ritwika Pal as Kia.

> **Watch the trailer and read the pitch.** Video

1 **Pick out the differences between the original story and the adaptation.**

2 **Give your point of view about this adaptation.**

BUILD YOUR PORTFOLIO

BAC

Julian Feder as Po and Christopher Gorham as his father.

Video

A BOY CALLED PO

A Boy Called Po (2016) is an American film directed by John Asher. It is about a relationship between a widower father and his autistic son. Asher's own son is autistic.

Watch the trailer and find the elements that echo *The Curious Incident of the Dog in the Night-Time.*

STUDYING AUTISM

Howard Buten is an American psychologist and clown (Buffo). He has worked on autism as a researcher, psychologist and founder of a clinic in Paris.

Much has been written about autism. I believe that this has to do with its mystery and its contradictions. The more we know about the little we've learned, the more mysterious and contradictory autism seems to become. Most sentences that begin, "Autistic people are…" will be necessarily false – there will always be some who aren't.

I began working with these astonishing people back in 1974. Nine years later I felt the need to write about them. I'm a writer; I write, I rewrote the first sentence for a year, trying to make it true, then gave up.

I spent the next twenty years scrupulously not writing the pages that you now hold in your hand. But what I did do during those years was ask myself why it was that I feel—have felt from the very beginning—so at home among the autistic. (Home: Where the heart is.) Many colleagues have asked me the same question. When I got tired of not being able to answer them, I decided to write the pages you now hold in your hand. I hoped they might provide me with a few answers.

Introduction, *Through the Glass Wall*, Howard Buten, 2005

1 **Read the introduction to Howard Buten's book and explain the difficulties related to writing about autism.**

2 **Account for the differences between an essay about autism and a work of fiction such as *The Curious Incident of the Dog in the Night-Time.***

THE REASON I JUMP

Many depictions of autism concentrate on "high-functioning" individuals. People with non-verbal forms of autism are much less visible or audible. Naoki Higashida published a memoir, *The Reason I Jump: The Inner Voice of a Thirteen-Year-Old Boy with Autism*, after his mother helped him communicate by pointing at characters on an alphabet board. The book was translated into English by novelist David Mitchell (*Cloud Atlas*) and his Japanese wife, KA Yoshida, because they had been very moved by it. They felt it gave them insight into their non-verbal autistic son's mind.

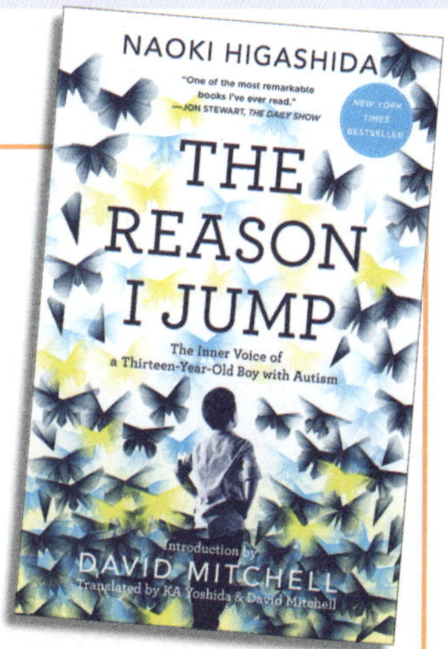

"Problem is, many children with autism don't have the means to express themselves, and often even their own parents don't have a clue what they might be thinking. So my big hope is that I can help a bit by explaining, in my own way, what's going on in the minds of people with autism. I also hope that, by reading this book, you might become a better friend of someone with autism."

The Reason I Jump (2007), Naoki Higashida

> What does *The Reason I Jump* deal with?

GOING FURTHER

Video

Carly Fleishman, a young American woman with autism who can't speak, has found social media is a great way to express herself. Watch this video where she explains what she experiences.

AUTISM ON TV

Video

Atypical is a comedy series that centres on Sam, a 19-year-old U.S. high-school student with autism who longs to date girls, just like his classmates.

The Good Doctor is a hospital drama series whose central character, student doctor Shaun Murphy, is on the autism spectrum but also has savant syndrome which means he has a perfect visual memory of medical diagrams and the workings of the human body.

Video

1 Look at the pictures, read the two pitches and watch the trailers. Is the approach similar?

2 Which one do you think is the most efficient to increase public awareness on autism?

Crédits des textes

5 Article by Mark Haddon. Reprinted by permission Penguin publishing, 2015
9, 12, 15, 18, 21, 23, 26, 28, 30, 33-34-36, 38-39, 44-43 Extracts of *From The Curious incident of the dog in the night-time* by Mark Haddon
Published by Vintage
Reprinted by permission of The Random House Group Limited. © 2004

Crédits photographiques

Couverture Mark Boutavent

3 et **4** PHOTO12.COM / ALAMY ; **5** Red Fox / Penguin UK ; **6** Vintage Random House/ Mark Boutavent ; **7** PHOTO12.COM / ALAMY ; **11** PHOTO12.COM ; **b** SHUTTERSTOCK/© mimony ; **12** et **13** SHUTTERSTOCK ; **14** Courtesy Very Well UK ; **16** BrinkhoffMögenburg ; **40** PHOTO12.COM / ALAMY / Lifestyle pictures ; **41** BrinkhoffMögenburg ; **46** BrinkhoffMögenburg ; **52h** BrinkhoffMögenburg ; **53h** BrinkhoffMögenburg ; **b** Ava Film Productions ; **54 h** Collection Christophel © Commonwealth Film Manufacturing / New Coast Productions ; **m** Vintage Books ; **b** GETTY IMAGES France / Gamma-Rapho / Hervé Bruhat ; **55 hg** © Miki Higashida ; **hd** Penguin Random House ; **bg** Netflix ; **bd** CHRISTOPHE L COLLECTION / © 3AD / ABC Studios / EnterMedia Content

N° de projet : 10265904 - Dépôt légal : décembre 2019
Achevé d'imprimé en juin 2020 par Estimprim